THE 12 WORST
FIRES OF ALL TIME

by Laura Perdew

12 STORY LIBRARY

www.12StoryLibrary.com

12-Story Library is an imprint of Bookstaves.

Photographs ©: Museum of London/CC, cover, 1; Yoshiharu Tashiro/CC, 4; CO Leong/Shutterstock.com, 5; Yale Center for British Art/CC, 6; AlexKozlov/iStockphoto, 7; Currier and Ives/Chicago History Museum/CC, 8; CC, 9; ZU_09/iStockphoto, 10; Greg Sanders/USFWS, 11; US Forest Service, 12; Library of Congress, 13; bradscottphotos/iStockphoto, 14; Fuatagabey/iStockphoto, 15; belfasteileen/iStockphoto, 16, 29; Doug James/Shutterstock.com, 17; mattmangum/CC2.0, 18; A. S. Zain/Shutterstock.com, 19; MODIS Rapid Response Team/NASA Earth Observatory, 20; Michalis Famelis/CC3.0, 21; Pheonix7777/CC4.0, 22; Bill Oxford/iStockphoto, 23; Nick carson/CC3.0, 24; CSIRO/CC3.0, 25; DarrenRD/CC4.0, 26; Joshua Stevens/NASA, 27

Data Library of Congress Cataloging-in-Publication
Names: Perdew, Laura, author
Title: The 12 worst fires of all time / by Laura Perdew.
Description: Mankato, MN : 12-Story Library, [2019] | Series: All-time worst disasters | Audience: Grades 3-5. | Includes index.
Identifiers: LCCN 2018011535 (print) | LCCN 2018013526 (ebook) | ISBN 9781632356543 (ebook) | ISBN 9781632355355 (hardcover : alk. paper) | ISBN 9781632356000 (pbk. : alk. paper)
Subjects: LCSH: Fires--History--Juvenile literature.
Classification: LCC TH9448 (ebook) | LCC TH9448 .P47 2019 (print) | DDC 363.3709--dc23
LC record available at https://lccn.loc.gov/2018011535

Printed in the United States of America
Mankato, MN
June 2018

About the Cover

An unknown artist's depiction of the Great Fire of London. The painting is in the style of the Dutch School and is not dated or signed.

12 STORY LIBRARY

Access free, up-to-date content on this topic plus a full digital version of this book. Scan the QR code on page 31 or use your school's login at 12StoryLibrary.com.

Table of Contents

1

Fire Sweeps Through Edo, Japan

The night of January 18, 1657, was very cold in Edo, Japan. Strong winds raced through the city from the north. People struggled to keep warm. According to legend, a fire began in a home. From there, it spread quickly. Flames consumed the wooden buildings crowded together on narrow streets. The wind fed the fire.

The winds were so fierce that people had little or no warning about the growing fire. Thousands were trapped. Many died trying to escape.

By the time firefighters were called out, the fire had spread across the city. The wind had driven it over two different rivers.

On January 19, the wind pushed the fire toward the Edo Castle. Several towers were burned. But firefighters saved the castle itself. The fire was finally contained on January 20. It continued to smolder for days.

The terrible blaze is known as the Great Fire of Meireki because it happened near the start of the

This handscroll painting of the Great Fire of Meireki dates back to 1814.

The Imperial Palace now stands on the former site of Edo Castle.

Meireki era in Japanese history. It destroyed about 60 percent of the city. Officials estimated that between 30,000 and 100,000 people died in the fire. Given the number of deaths, individual burials were impossible. Pits were dug for the dead. Monks said prayers for individuals as they were placed in the pits. Once covered, a memorial hall was built over the mass graves. It is called the *Eko-In*, which means "Temple of Prayer for the Dead."

2

Number of years it took to rebuild Edo after the fire.

- Once the fire started, it spread quickly between the wooden buildings.
- Tens of thousands of people died trying to escape.
- The fire threatened the Edo Castle, but firefighters were able to save it.
- The dead were buried in mass graves.

2

Panic Reigns in the Great Fire of London

The Great Fire of London, England, began in the early morning of September 2, 1666. The summer had been extremely hot and dry. The wooden houses and buildings of the city were dry, too. When a fire began in the kitchen of the king's baker, it grew quickly. The fire spread from the bakery to the next building. And the next. As fire jumped from house to house, people tried to put out the flames with buckets of water. Even the king, Charles II, joined the effort.

As the fire grew, people panicked. Londoners ran through the city streets, trying to escape. Many

Philippe-Jacques de Loutherbourg painted this depiction of the Great London Fire in 1797.

A monument to the Great Fire stands by the London Bridge today.

REBUILDING LONDON

It took 50 years to rebuild the city after the Great Fire. The first year was spent clearing the burned area. Time was also taken to plan how the streets would be laid out. New building regulations were set up to prevent future fire disasters. The streets were made wider. Once rebuilt, London was thought to be among the finest cities in the world.

went to the Thames River to try to flee by boat. King Charles II ordered firefighters to create a firebreak. Houses in the path of the fire were pulled down with hooked poles. But wind kept the fire moving. Days later, the king ordered that houses in the path of the fire be blown up using gunpowder. This created more panic. People thought London was being invaded by the French.

By the time the flames were put out on September 6, 80 percent of London had burned. Over 13,000 buildings were destroyed. Tens of thousands of people were left homeless. But fewer than 10 people died.

5

Number of days London burned before the fire was extinguished.

- The fire started in the king's bakery.
- It spread quickly through the city of dry wooden buildings.
- Eighty percent of London burned.

3

Huge Blaze Leaves Chicago in Ruins

In October 1871, the city of Chicago, Illinois, desperately needed rain. Drought gripped the city. Everything was very dry, including Chicago's many wooden buildings. When a barn erupted in flames on October 8, fire quickly spread to nearby shanties and sheds. Neighbors rushed out of their homes to try to stop the blaze. They opened fire hydrants on the street to get water and used buckets to carry it to the flames.

Despite neighbors' efforts, the heat and size of the fire grew. Wind whipped the blaze into walls of flame. Some flames reached 100 feet (30 m) into the air. The whirls of fire, called fire devils, moved across the city. All fire engines were called. But the heat was so fierce it

People ran for their lives to escape the flames.

Map of the burned area. The circle shows where the fire started.

was hard for firefighters to stand near the flames.

Rain helped to put out the fire two days later. By that time, the Great Chicago Fire had burned one-third of the city. Approximately 18,000 buildings were destroyed. Streets and sidewalks made of wood were also burned up. As many as 300 people lost their lives. Witnesses described a city in total ruin.

COW CAUSES FIRE?

There is a song that blames a cow for knocking over a lantern and starting the fire. The truth is, no one knows how the fire started. Some people blamed Mrs. O'Leary, the woman who owned the barn and the cow. Others thought they saw someone from a nearby party go into the barn. Or maybe a spark from a neighbor's chimney blew onto the O'Learys' barn. The true cause remains a mystery.

100,000

Number of people left homeless following the fire.

- The Great Chicago Fire started in a barn and spread to neighboring buildings.
- Drought and wind fueled the fire through a city built mostly of wood.
- One-third of Chicago was burned.

4 Fleeing Fire, Wisconsin Townspeople Dive into River

In 1871, Peshtigo, Wisconsin, was a small town surrounded by thick forest. That summer, the region experienced a drought. The forests were tinder-dry. Wooden homes, stores, barns, and boardwalks were dry, too.

Many small wildfires affected the area that summer and fall. Ash fell from the sky. Smoke was thick in the air. School was even closed some days. On the night of October 8, winds from a cold front blew the small fires into one massive fire. The column of hot air from the blaze combined with the cooler air above. The updraft created a firenado, a tornado of fire.

By 10:00 p.m., all of Peshtigo was on fire. The air was full of smoke, ash, sparks, and dust. Hurricane-force winds knocked people over and uprooted trees. Residents tried to flee in all directions, clogging the

Townspeople sought safety in the river to escape the flames.

streets. Many sought refuge in a nearby river. People jumped in the water to escape the flames.

The Great Peshtigo Fire destroyed the town of Peshtigo and burned 16 others in the surrounding area. Peshtigo was the hardest hit. The fast-moving fire burned the town to the ground in an hour. In that town alone, 800 people died. Over a million acres were burned in the region.

2,000

Approximate number of people living in Peshtigo in 1870.

- Weather conditions created fire tornadoes.
- There was chaos in the streets as people tried to outrun the flames.
- In Peshtigo, 800 people lost their lives.

SURVIVAL IN THE WATER

Many of the Peshtigo residents who sought safety in the river could not swim. They had to choose between the fire and the water. Even in the river, people were in danger as the flames licked over them. They had to keep wetting their heads. The water was very cold in October. One survivor spent more than five and a half hours in the river.

Heat from a fire combined with cooler air creates a firenado.

5 Wildfire Scorches Millions of Acres in Rockies

The summer of 1910 was very dry in Idaho, Montana, and Washington. The states received no more than an inch of rain all summer. Many small wildfires burned during these dry months. Lightning started some. Sparks from passing trains ignited others. On August 20, hurricane-force winds whipped through Idaho. The smaller fires merged together into an inferno. Crews that had been battling the smaller fires ran for their lives. Seventy-eight crewmembers didn't make it out.

Winds of 75 miles per hour (120 km/h) uprooted trees and tossed them aside like matches. Bits of burning wood were blown as far as 10 miles. Flaming embers rained from the sky. Nothing in the path of the blaze was spared. Witnesses said the fire roared like a furnace. At one point, the wall of fire was reported to be 50 miles wide (80 km). Heat from the blaze made the air difficult to breathe. Smoke darkened the sky and turned day into night. The smog could be seen as far away as New York City.

After two days, the fire burned itself out. The blaze was called the Big Burn because of its power and the widespread damage it caused.

Ranger Ed Pulaski and 40 of his men survived the fire in an abandoned mineshaft.

Aftermath of the wildfire and hurricane-force winds in Coeur d'Alene, Idaho.

3 million

Number of acres (1,214,057 hectares) the Big Burn scorched in Idaho, Washington, and Montana.

- Smaller fires were whipped into one big inferno by hurricane-force wind.
- Fire crews could not stop the inferno.
- The fire took the lives of 78 firefighters.

6 Black Dragon Fire Roars Across China and Siberia

In May 1987, the Black Dragon Fire consumed 18 million acres (7,284,342 hectares) of forest in China and Siberia. The land was very dry due to below-average snowfall the previous winter. Disaster struck on May 6. That's when a spark from brush-cutting equipment ignited a fire in northeast China.

Soon walls of flame swept through the forest. The fire burned on both sides of the Amur River, which separates China and the Siberia. The worst days of the fire were May 7 and 8. On those two days, the fire killed approximately 200 people. It injured hundreds more.

China did not have much firefighting equipment. The government sent two army troops and forest workers to fight the fire. Approximately 60,000 people fought to preserve the forest. On the other side of the river, Russia took a different approach. They let the fire burn.

A spark from brush-cutting equipment started the fire.

In June, the wind slackened. Rain helped to contain the fire. But not before it had burned three million acres (1,214,057 hectares) in China and 15 million acres (6,070,285 hectares) in Siberia. The total area burned is the size of New England in the United States.

30

Percentage of the Black Dragon Forest that burned in China.

- A spark from brush-cutting equipment started the fire.
- The fire was fought on the Chinese side of the river, but not the Siberian side.
- A total of 18 million acres (7,284,342 hectares) burned.

THINK ABOUT IT

The loss of so many trees in the Black Dragon Fire caused great damage to the ecology of the forest. How was the ecology of the area changed? Has the environment recovered?

7

Summer of Fire Torches Yellowstone National Park

The summer 1988 tourism season in Yellowstone National Park began like most others. But the previous winters had been unusually dry. The summer brought hot and dry weather. The conditions were perfect for wildfires. The first of many fires began on June 14. Over the next months, more than 50 different wildfires began. Lightning strikes from storms started most of the blazes. Others were accidentally caused by park visitors.

At first, the National Park Service let some of the fires burn. Wildfires are part of the healthy management of forests. Crews put out other fires that threatened people and buildings. But strong winds picked up and rapidly spread the flames. The firestorm advanced up to 10 miles on some days. Rangers began to worry that all of Yellowstone would be destroyed.

Helicopters and airplanes dropped water on the fire. Thousands of firefighters from all over the United States fought flames on

Forest fire clouds in Yellowstone National Park.

the ground. Military personnel were also called in to help. In all, approximately 25,000 people battled the fire. It was the largest firefighting effort in US history. The cost to fight the blazes was $120 million.

Fires burned for three months. On September 11, rain and snow fell over Yellowstone. The precipitation, combined with cooler weather, helped officials to finally contain the flames. By then, fire had burned approximately 36 percent of the park. No human lives were lost, but several hundred large animals died.

200

Feet into the air (61 m) some of the flames reached.

- More than 50 different fires were burning in Yellowstone.
- Strong winds made the fires worse.
- Approximately 25,000 people fought the fire.

THE LAND RECOVERS

Wildfires are a natural part of the Yellowstone ecosystem. While the 1988 fires burned much of the park, they did not destroy it. Instead, new plants emerged quickly after the fire. They were fed by the ash, which contains minerals. More sunlight also reached the forest floor. Pine trees, aspen, birds, and animals all thrived following the fire.

Trees, plants, and animals have thrived following the 1988 fire.

8

Smoke from Wildfires Chokes Southeast Asia

In some parts of the world, fire is used to clear fields for farming. This slash-and-burn technique helps people produce more food. But it can also lead to disaster. That's what happened in Indonesia in late 1997, when drought and high temperatures led some of these fires to get out of control.

The wildfires spread quickly. Many were difficult for firefighters to reach, so they continued to burn. Soon smoke from blazes reached nearby countries. The haze was so thick in some places that it blocked the sun and fruit crops couldn't ripen. Transportation was affected. Low visibility led

to boat accidents. Some airports closed. Millions of people had health problems because of the smog.

The fires and haze continued into 1998. When the flames were finally extinguished, as many as 20 million acres (8,093,713 hectares) had burned. An economic disaster, the fires cost approximately $5 billion. They also impacted the environment. Carbon dioxide (CO_2) released into the atmosphere caused pollution levels to hit record highs. In addition, fires hurt biodiversity in affected areas.

2.5

Gigatons of carbon dioxide produced by fires around the world each year—equal to 40 percent of annual global emissions.

- The fires in Southeast Asia were caused by people burning land to clear it for farming.
- The haze and smog from the fire caused problems around the region.
- The fires burned as many as 20 million acres (8,093,713 hectares).

THINK ABOUT IT

The pollution and smog from the fires were so bad that people were warned to stay indoors or to use surgical masks if they went out. What health problems might breathing that polluted air cause?

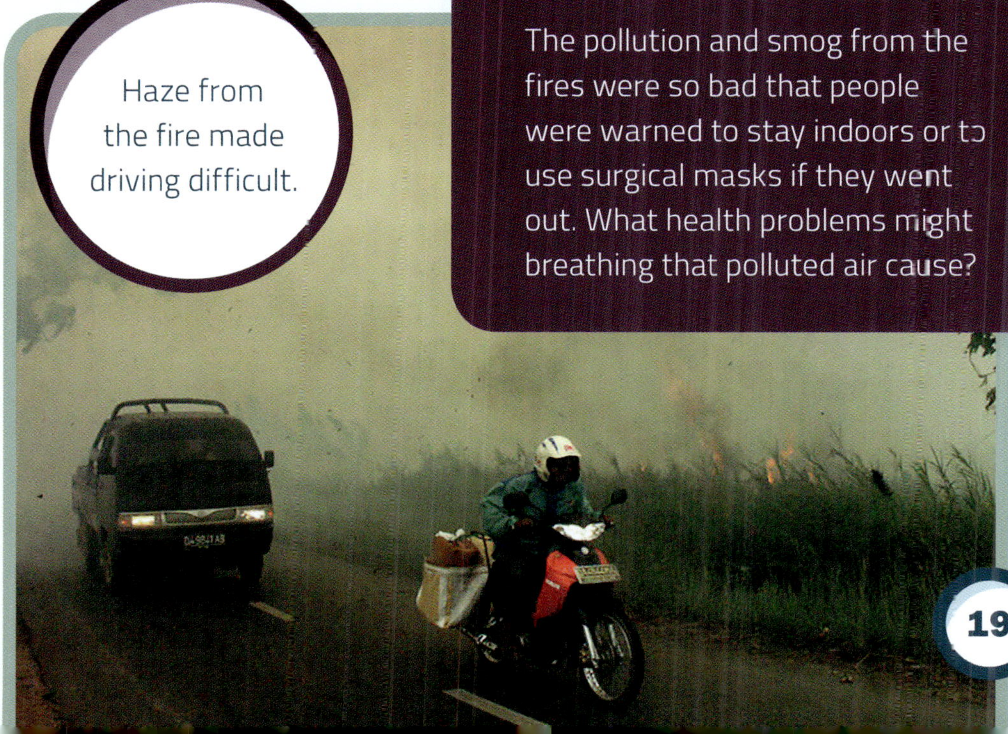

Haze from the fire made driving difficult.

9

Wildfires Char Greek Forests and Farmlands

The summer of 2007 was the hottest on record in Greece. The country was also in a drought. These conditions led to one of the country's worst wildfire seasons. The first blaze started in June. Officials believe a downed electrical line ignited it. Lightning strikes and arsonists started other fires.

The fires quickly spread. They were pushed on by high wind. Greek firefighters battled the flames. Soon, though, the fires were out of control. The country's prime minister declared a state of emergency and asked for help from other countries. Special firefighting airplanes, helicopters, and personnel from around Europe were sent to Greece. The Greek military helped fight the fires, too.

Battling the flames took all summer. August was the most dangerous month. More than 60 people died from fires during that period. Thousands more had to leave their homes. Many people were trapped in villages surrounded by fire. At last, on September 3, the flames were put out by fire crews.

Throughout the summer, approximately 3,000 different fires raged across Greece. An estimated 670,000 acres (271,139 hectares) burned. Many laurel, oak, and pine forests were lost. Villages, farms, and olive groves also burned. A total of 84 people lost their lives.

Clouds of smoke captured by NASA's Aqua satellite.

Thousands of people had to evacuate their homes.

110

Number of villages razed by the flames.

- Lightning, electrical lines, and arsonists caused the fires.
- The Greek fires spread quickly because of the heat and drought.
- The prime minister declared a state of emergency and asked for foreign aid.

10 California Suffers Worst Wildfire Season on Record

In the early months of 2017, California received above-average rainfall. Precipitation spurred the growth of grasses and other vegetation. However, the following summer was hot and arid. The vegetation dried out. When strong Santa Ana winds stirred up in the fall, conditions were perfect for wildfires.

In Northern California, more than a dozen fires ignited in October. Starting within a few days of each other, they roared across the region in an unstoppable inferno. Flames torched neighborhoods, forests, vineyards, and farmlands. People in seven counties were evacuated. The Tubbs Fire alone destroyed 5,643 structures and burned nearly 37,000 acres (14,973 hectares). It ranked as the most destructive individual blaze by cost in state history.

The 2017 wildfire season was the worst in California history.

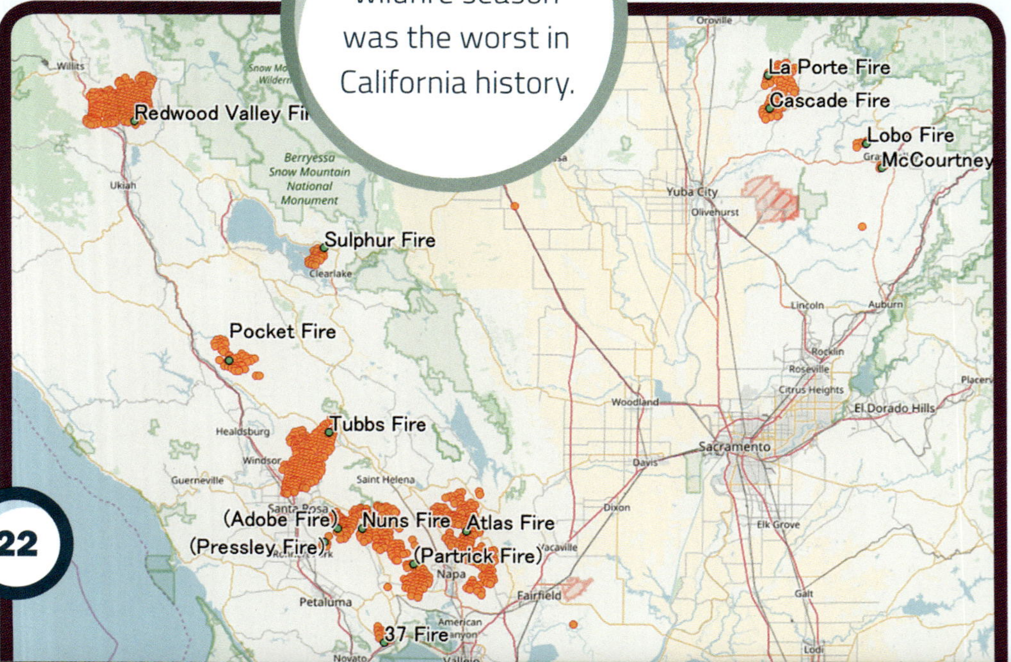

A housing complex of over 1,000 homes was burned in one night.

December rainfall usually brings an end to the Californian fire season. However, in 2017, conditions remained dry. Extreme winds persisted. Early in the month, fires broke out in Southern California.

One was the Thomas Fire, which became the largest wildfire by area in state history. The blaze charred over 281,000 acres (113,717 hectares) and destroyed more than 1,000 structures before it was fully contained.

The 2017 wildfire season was the worst in California history. In total, 1.2 million acres (485,223 hectares) burned during the course of the year.

5,700

Approximate number of homes destroyed.

- The Tubbs Fire was the most destructive fire by cost in California history.
- The Thomas Fire was the largest wildfire by area.
- In 2017, 1.2 million acres (485,223 hectares) burned across California

THINK ABOUT IT

Fighting the California wildfires was difficult and dangerous. How can people prevent such fires from starting?

11

Black Saturday Bushfires Ravage Australian Landscape

Fires in the dry parts of the Australian bush are normal. But the Black Saturday bushfires on February 7, 2009, were anything but normal. Before that day, the southern state of Victoria had experienced the worst heat wave in 100 years. Temperatures exceeded 117 degrees Fahrenheit (47.2°C). The humidity was very low. Vegetation was extremely dry. Downed power lines, lightning, and arsonists had already sparked several small fires in the state.

On February 7, strong winds whipped existing fires into a firestorm. Flames raced across the state. Residents had no warning about what was coming. Some described the blaze as a rolling ball of fire that sped toward them. People fled with the fire at their backs. Some died in their cars trying to escape. Others had burns on the soles of their feet.

Thousands of firefighters fought blazes on the ground. Firefighting aircraft dropped water on the fires from the air. It took weeks of

Smoke from the bushfires in Yarra Ranges National Park could be seen for miles.

firefighting to finally put out the fires. By the time the smoke cleared, 173 people had died. Hundreds more were injured. Seventy-eight towns were affected and approximately 7,500 people were left homeless.

ACCOUNTABILITY AFTER THE BLAZE

After the fires, lawsuits were filed against the electric company responsible for the downed power lines. The company settled for almost $800 million. In addition, one man was convicted of arson and sent to prison. The people of Victoria were devastated by the fires. Many people had lost loved ones, pets, and homes. Doctors and psychologists found that many people continued to struggle long after the fires were out.

400

Number of individual fires that burned in Victoria on Black Saturday.

- Record heat, low humidity, and strong winds created the perfect conditions for fire.
- The blaze was so fast and so intense people described it as a rolling ball of fire.
- 173 people died, many in their cars as they tried to escape.

12

"The Beast" Rages in Alberta

On May 1, 2016, a small wildfire started southwest of the town of Fort McMurray, Alberta, Canada. Within hours, air tankers carrying water arrived in the area. Nearby residents were told to prepare to evacuate. The blaze grew on May 2. Still, firefighters believed the fire to be under control.

Then on May 3, temperatures spiked and the humidity dipped. The wind shifted. The fire exploded. Blue skies turned black with smoke. Residents were ordered to evacuate. People grabbed whatever they could and fled. Roads were clogged with cars as the towering walls of flame advanced.

The fire did most of its damage to Fort McMurray in its first few days. Flames consumed 2,400 buildings, though firefighters saved 25,000 others. There were no deaths. After passing

88,000 people were forced to leave their homes.

through Fort McMurray, the fire continued to burn out of control in the wilderness areas outside the city for another month. By the time it was contained on July 4, the blaze had burned almost 2,317 square miles (6,000 square kilometers). Because of its size and strength, the Fort McMurray fire was nicknamed "The Beast." The exact cause of the fire is unknown, but officials have ruled out lightning and believe it was human caused.

A NASA satellite image shows the wildfire burning through Fort McMurray.

A LASTING IMPACT

One year after the fire swept through Fort McMurray, the town was still recovering. Some residents never returned. Others were rebuilding. Those who went back pulled together, bonded by the experience. The fire itself burned throughout the winter. One year later, it was still smoldering in the remote wilderness east of Fort McMurray.

8,000

Number of people evacuated from Fort McMurray.

- Within two days, a small wildfire southwest of Fort McMurray became a massive wall of flames that hit the town.
- The entire town was evacuated.
- Many homes were lost, but no one died.
- The fire burned almost 2,317 square miles (6,000 square kilometers).

Staying Safe If There Is a Fire

At Home:

- Install smoke detectors in several locations. Check them regularly to make sure they are working. Replace batteries twice a year.
- Have an evacuation plan in place. Identify at least two different ways to exit each room.
- In the event of a fire, leave immediately. If there is smoke, stay low to the ground. Never open a door if the knob is hot. Once outside, stay outside—never go back into a building.
- Create an outdoor meeting place where everyone can gather if a fire occurs.
- Practice fire drills at home.

Wildfires:

- People living in areas prone to wildfires should make an evacuation plan that includes at least two ways to escape. In the plan, include how to contact friends and family.
- Be ready to evacuate on short notice. Have a checklist of items to take if forced to leave quickly (including medicines and food).

- Families with pets should know how to prepare animals for transport. Pet food should be on the evacuation checklist.
- In the event of a nearby wildfire, obey evacuation orders by firefighters and police.
- People living in an area affected by smoke from a wildfire should limit outdoor activities to protect their health.

Glossary

arson
The criminal act of purposely setting fire to property.

biodiversity
The wide variety of different species that live on Earth.

bush
In Australia, vast unsettled areas covered by scrub and forest.

drought
Extended periods of below-average precipitation.

evacuate
To leave an unsafe area and find a place of safety.

firebreak
An area cleared of vegetation in the path of the fire meant to stop it from advancing.

firestorm
A wildfire of extreme heat and size, usually driven by intense wind.

ignite
To start a fire.

inferno
A large fire that is dangerous and out of control.

shanties
Roughly built huts or shacks.

slash-and-burn
The method of clearing land for farming with fire.

tinder
Something that is very dry and flammable.

updraft
A current of air that moves upward.

For More Information

Books

Adamson, Thomas K., and Heather Adamson. *California Wildfires Survival Stories.* Natural Disaster True Survival Stories. Troy, MI: Momentum Books, 2016.

Bell, Samantha S. *Detecting Wildfires.* Detecting Disasters Series. Burnsville, MN: Focus Readers Publishing, 2017.

Kavanagh, James. *Wildfire Survival: Prepare For & Survive a Wildfire.* Urban Survival Series. Tampa, FL: Waterford Press, 2015.

Simon, Seymour. *Wildfires.* New York: HarperCollins Publishers, 2016.

Index

About the Author

Laura Perdew is an author, writing consultant, and former middle school teacher. She writes fiction and nonfiction for children, including many titles for the education market. Laura lives and plays in Boulder, Colorado.